PETS IN THE WILD!

BEARDED DRAGONS IN THE WILD!

by Grace Hansen

Cody Koala
An Imprint of Pop!
popbooksonline.com

Hello! My name is Cody Koala

This book is filled with videos, puzzles, games, and more! Scan the QR codes* while you read, or visit the website below to make this book pop.

popbooksonline.com/b-dragon

*Scanning QR codes requires a web-enabled smart device with a QR code reader app and a camera.

abdobooks.com
Published by Pop!, a division of ABDO, PO Box 398166, Minneapolis, Minnesota 55439.

Printed in the United States of America, North Mankato, Minnesota.
052024
092024

THIS BOOK CONTAINS RECYCLED MATERIALS

Cover Photo: Shutterstock Images
Interior Photos: Shutterstock Images, Getty Images
Editor: Elizabeth Andrews
Series Designer: Laura Graphenteen; Neil Klinepier

Library of Congress Control Number: 2023947437

Publisher's Cataloging-in-Publication Data
Names: Hansen, Grace, author.
Title: Bearded dragons in the wild! / by Grace Hansen
Description: Minneapolis, Minnesota : Pop!, 2025 | Series: Pets in the wild! | Includes online resources and index
Identifiers: ISBN 9781098246112 (lib. bdg.) | ISBN 9781098246679 (ebook)
Subjects: LCSH: Bearded dragons (Reptiles)--Juvenile literature. | Lizards--Juvenile literature. | Reptiles--Juvenile literature. | Wild animals--Juvenile literature.
Classification: DDC 636.0887--dc23

Table of Contents

Chapter 1

Bearded Dragons

Bearded dragons are lizards. They get their name for the spiny scales on their throats. When a bearded dragon feels **threatened**, its throat darkens in color and puffs up. It looks like a beard!

Watch a video here!

Bearded dragons are **omnivores**. They have strong jaws to crush the shells of insects. They also eat plants and animals such as small lizards.

Bearded dragons are also called "beardies."

Chapter 2

Bearded Dragons in the Wild

There are eight bearded dragon **species**. They are found in areas throughout Australia. They live in **habitats** such as deserts and shrublands.

Where Wild Bearded Dragons Live

Learn more here!

Bearded dragons are good climbers. They climb trees to find food and bask in the sun.

Bearded dragons are cold-blooded animals. They rely on the sun's rays for warmth. They can often be seen **basking** in the sun.

When temperatures are too hot, bearded dragons move underground to stay cool. This also keeps them safe from **predators**.

Chapter 3

Pet Bearded Dragons

Bearded dragons make wonderful pets. The central bearded dragon is the most common **species** to have as a pet. They are gentle and curious. They like being around their owners.

Explore links here!

Chapter 4

Caring for Bearded Dragons

Bearded dragons are usually easy to care for. The most important thing is that they have a clean, safe **enclosure** that is large enough for their size.

Complete an activity here!

Bearded dragons should have lots of room to move. Their enclosures should also have proper lighting and heating. It is also important that they have a place to **bask** on and hide in.

Adult bearded dragons are usually 16 to 24 inches (41-61cm) long.

Pet bearded dragons should be fed a good diet. They enjoy vegetables and insects, such as cucumbers and crickets. They can also

eat an occasional piece of apple. Bearded dragons that are well cared for can live eight to 12 years or more!

Making Connections

Text-to-Self

What is your favorite thing about bearded dragons?

Text-to-Text

Have you read any other books about bearded dragons? What did you learn in those books that was not in this one?

Text-to-World

Australia is home to lots of animals, including wild bearded dragons. What other animals do you like that live in Australia?

Glossary

bask – to lie in a warm, calm place.

enclosure – a type of secure container meant to keep a pet animal safe.

habitat – the natural environment of an animal or plant.

omnivore – an animal that eats both plants and other animals.

predator – an animal that hunts other animals for food.

species – animals that look alike and can have young together.

threatened – having an uncertain chance of surviving into the future.

Index

Online Resources

popbooksonline.com

Thanks for reading this Cody Koala book!

This book is filled with videos, puzzles, games, and more! Scan the QR codes* while you read, or visit the website below to make this book pop.

popbooksonline.com/b-dragon

*Scanning QR codes requires a web-enabled smart device with a QR code reader app and a camera.